NOT IN VAIN

Not in vain
may be the pride of those who survived
and the epitaph of those who fell.

WINSTON CHURCHILL

NOT IN

VAIN

Photographs Ken Bell
Text   C. P. Stacey
Captions   Kildare Dobbs

David & Charles

0 7153 5855 3

© University of Toronto Press

Printed in Great Britain by
Sir Joseph Causton & Sons Ltd London & Eastleigh
for David & Charles (Holdings) Limited
South Devon House Newton Abbot Devon

Contents

Preface

The experience of fighting in western Europe and then travelling again over roads and countryside that were the scene of previous war has been shared by many people over many generations. For me, it began on D-Day when I went ashore, attached to the Highland Light Infantry of Canada, carrying my Rolleiflex camera, a lieutenant in the Film and Photo Section of the Canadian Army. In a subsequent career as a professional photographer, I was able to go back and see and record what was happening as the scars of war were repaired and as, at the same time, Europe came to lose so much trace of all the stir and devastation and death that occurred in 1944 and 1945. In *Curtain Call*, published in 1953, I tried to show the changes brought by man and nature in the five years since VE day; and in this book are portrayed and contrasted the scenes of battle and of peace at an interval of twenty-five years. To some it will recall their own experiences, and to others, I hope, it will say something of the nature and significance of the last war in Europe.

In compiling this collection of photographs, I was greatly assisted by the generous co-operation of the Public Archives of Canada and by my able and faithful assistant, Joyce Lees. I am grateful too to Hilary Marshall and Rik Davidson of the University of Toronto Press, to Ian Williams of David & Charles, and to Guy Simonds, C P Stacey, and Kildare Dobbs for providing the verbal counterpoint to the photographs.

And to the people of France, Belgium, and Holland who have given me such a warm welcome on all my visits, this book will express, I hope, something of my gratitude for their strong and warm humanity.

KEN BELL

7

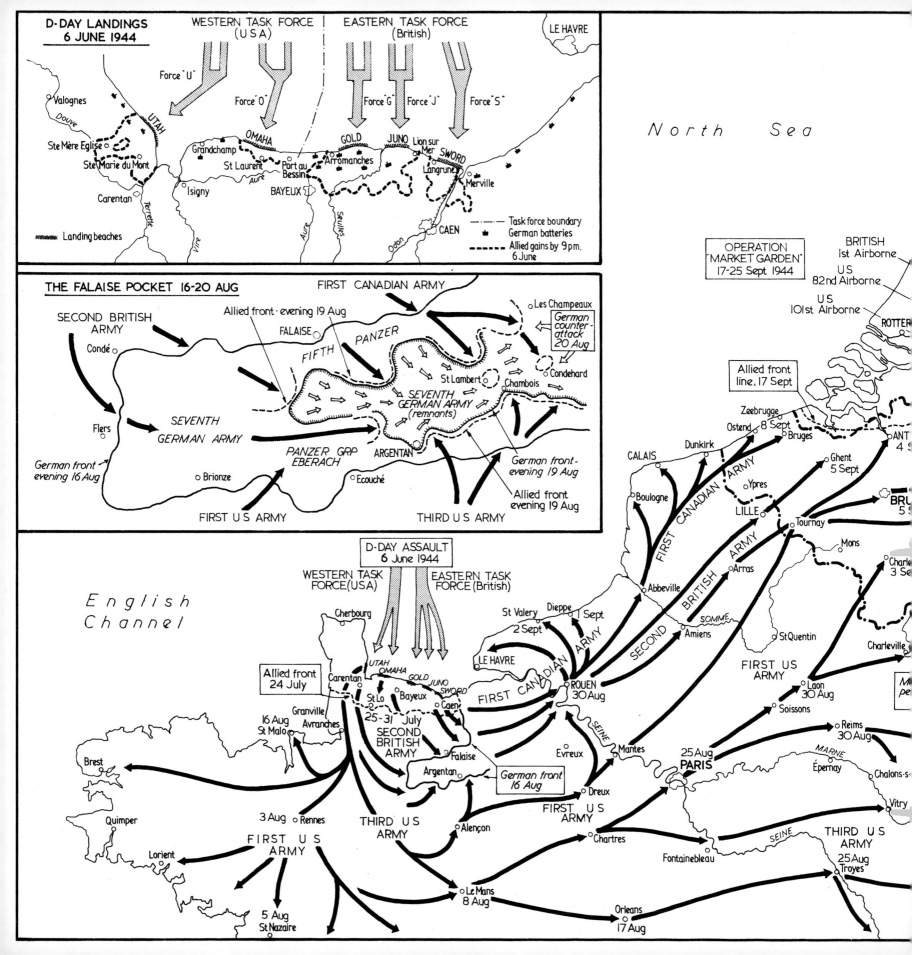

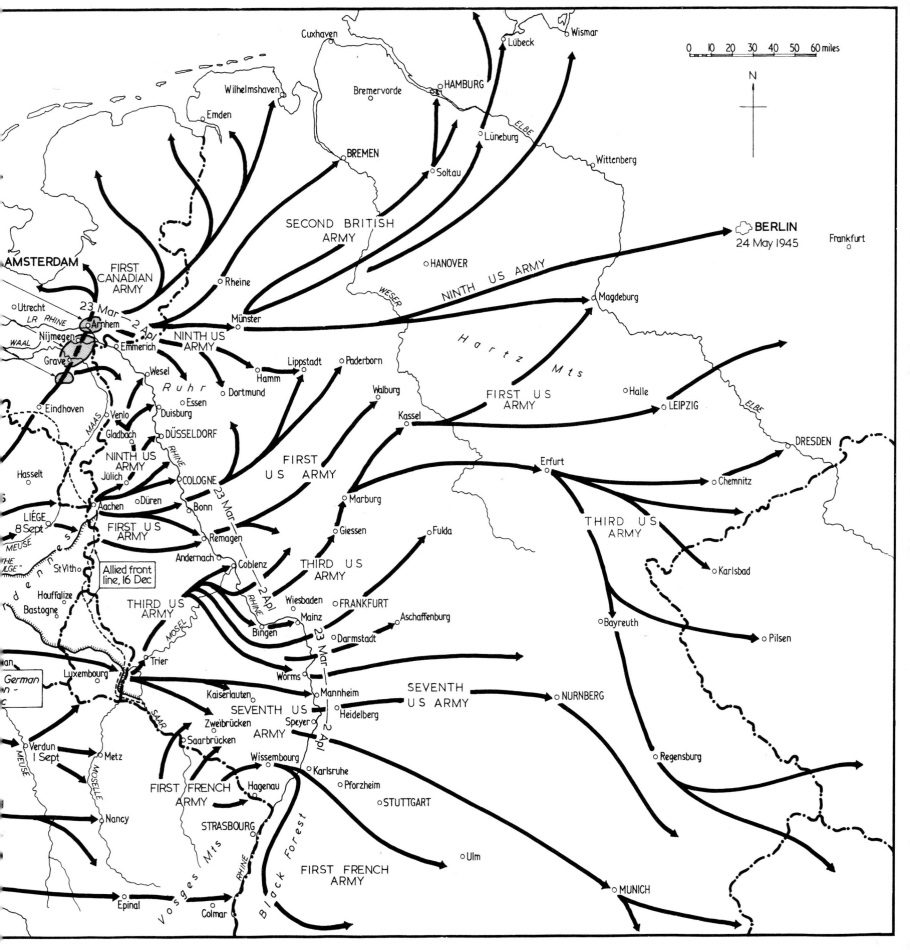

Part I
Normandy

Some of us who lived through those times find it a little hard to believe that it is well over a quarter of a century since General Eisenhower's armies stormed ashore in Normandy on 6 June 1944. That day, so long awaited by the Allied peoples, was the beginning of a campaign which in eleven months carried the soldiers of the Western Allies to the shores of the Baltic, ruined Adolf Hitler's Third Reich which he had boasted would last a thousand years, and also spelled the doom of the imperialists of Japan.

Years had been devoted to planning the Normandy invasion. Many nations contributed to the assault, but it was mainly the work of three. Two United States divisions, and part of a third, landed from the sea on the right, a Canadian division in the centre, and two British divisions on the left. The command was shared between the First US Army, under Lieut-General Omar N Bradley, and the Second British Army under Lieut-General M C Dempsey. On the far western flank, two American airborne divisions dropped from the sky; on the eastern side, a British airborne division —which included a Canadian battalion—parachuted down. Great naval and air forces chiefly provided by the same three countries prepared the way for the attack and supported it.

The Germans had long been expecting an invasion. Since the summer of 1942 they had been constructing the strong system of beach defences called the Atlantic Wall. But their generals were not in agreement on the way to meet the coming assault. Field-Marshal Gerd von Rundstedt, the sagacious old Commander-in-Chief West, believed that the defence must depend primarily on the classic method, mobile counter-attack by armoured divisions held back in reserve for the purpose.

His younger subordinate, Field-Marshal Erwin Rommel, commanding Army Group B in the Netherlands, Belgium, and Northern France, took the contrary view that Allied air superiority (of which he had had painful experience in North Africa) would prevent such large movements of reserves. He considered that the battle would be lost or won by the troops holding the beaches and the reserves locally available; and at the end of 1943 he set to work to encumber the beaches in his area with great numbers of mines and obstacles. Looking back, it is hard to say that either Rommel or von Rundstedt was right or wrong; under the conditions of 1944 their problem was insoluble.

The Germans were ignorant of the time and place of the invasion. Though there are some indications that just before it took place Rommel became apprehensive of an attack in Normandy, their heaviest concentration of force was not there but facing the Strait of Dover. And when we landed in Normandy Rommel himself was at his home in Germany, on his way to a meeting with Hitler. The defending forces were totally surprised.

The D-Day battle on 6 June was a great Allied victory. Rommel's 'asparagus' on the beaches did not stop our landing craft, and the Atlantic Wall was broken in a single summer morning. On one American beach there was bloody fighting, on the other virtually none. All along their front the British and Canadians met fierce resistance, but the issue was never really in doubt. The Allies' losses were heavy, but not so heavy as had been feared. Within four days the separate bridgeheads had joined up into one solid position, and it was clear that the invaders were on the Continent to stay. But the Germans had reacted with their usual violence and resolution, and particularly on the eastern flank where they instantly decided that the city of Caen was the key of their defence, they dug in their heels and fought desperately. The British had hoped to take Caen on D-Day, but did not succeed; there was a damaging counter-attack against the Canadians west of the city on D plus one; and a month of bitter toe-to-toe fighting followed before the Anglo-Canadian forces entered Caen, after a final costly two-day battle, on 9 July.

To General Sir Bernard Montgomery, who was commanding the whole Allied ground force for the initial phase of the campaign, these developments were not entirely unwelcome. His plan was to draw the enemy's main strength on to the eastern or British flank of the bridgehead, and thus to facilitate a break-out by the Americans in the west. The Germans co-operated by concentrating the great mass of their armour around Caen. This was hard on the British and Canadians, but it was what the plan required. During June the US troops captured Cherbourg and cleared the Cherbourg peninsula. Through July the hard slugging around Caen continued. By the 25th the Americans in the west were in position for the break-out. That day, aided by a tremendous blow by Allied heavy bombers, they launched their offensive ('the main blow of the whole Allied plan', Montgomery called it) in the area of St Lô. By the end of the month they were in Avranches ready to burst into Brittany. General George S Patton's Third US Army now entered the battle in this sector and set off upon a great turning movement in the direction of Paris intended to force the enemy back against the Seine. At the same time General H D G Crerar's First Canadian Army likewise took over a sector below Caen and was ordered to launch a heavy attack southward towards Falaise. This was to be the break-out from the bridgehead on the eastern flank.

Characteristically, Adolf Hitler now took a hand himself. To the consternation of his generals, the amateur strategist gave orders that a great German tank force was to be collected and hurled westward towards Avranches, with the object of driving through to the sea and cutting Patton's communications. Four panzer divisions went in to the attack on the night of 6–7 August. They failed. The Americans on the ground met them resolutely; and on 7 August, in perfect flying weather, the Allied tactical air forces struck a series of blows that stopped the offensive in its tracks. The defeat of this rash westward thrust exposed many of the most formidable and valuable units in the German Army to encirclement as Patton's columns swept east.

Time and tides have washed away the scars of battle here at Courseulles in Normandy. A man digs clams as dawn lights up the east. An old woman knits in gentle sunlight. The waves murmur and sigh but there is no grief here today. The people are at peace. Here on the windy morning of June 6, 1944, soldiers stormed in from the sea to drive out the Germans.

14

Along the coast the guns of Arromanches, silenced forever,
recall the bloody past.

Part of 'Fortress Europe's' Atlantic wall, these guns
were put out of action by seaborne invaders.

17

Approaching the Norman shore between Ouistreham and the neck of the Cherbourg peninsula. An allied armada of 5300 vessels supported by 12,000 planes has carried the soldiers over the sea from England. Many are seasick from the rough crossing. And now there is the tension of H-hour approaching in the chill light of dawn.

A child runs barefoot in over the seawashed sand.

At high water the first wave of landing craft ran aground and lowered ramps. The sea has receded by now, leaving them stranded. Follow-up troops trudge over the sand to join the battle for the bridgehead.

22

The first amphibious tank to swim ashore at Courseulles and make its way inland. After the war its Canadian commander, Sergeant Leo Gariepy, came back to Courseulles to stay. He looks after public works now.

Cycling is not very dangerous in Ouistreham today.

Free French Infantry advance along the same street.

Captured Germans are brought to the railway platform at
Bernières-sur-mer, back of Nan beach just east of
Courseulles. The railway station survives—as a bus depot.

24

The beaches are quiet now, where a man and his dog dig for shellfish. There was a time when it was not so quiet: dazed German survivors of bombardment and battle are marched to captivity.

Relic of the pride of Hitler's Third Reich, a bastion of the
Atlantic Wall. One of its captors grins while a comrade, less
lucky, is helped to safety by two others, his shattered face
muffled in a field dressing. Stretcher bearers carry away a third.
Victory is bought with blood.

Prisoners and their captors are departed, to die in battle or in bed. Tides have ebbed and flowed, silting up the breakwater. A row of bathing huts replaces the barbed wire. And if strangers come again, it will be to swim or fish.

How beautiful they are, the green fields and farms of Normandy. From these pastures, centuries ago, came the Norman ancestors of many of the soldiers who fought and died here in 1944. Along the road whose poplars cross the horizon soldiers marched inland to the agony of Caen. The cattle doze as if nothing had happened.

This was the road they travelled, bursting walls with their
gunfire, shattering the country peace with the tumult of their
tanks and trucks and jeeps. They travelled the road and moved
on to victory or wounds or death. And then the rain washed out
their tracks and the country was itself again.

The soldier's shovel saves his life more often than his rifle. Like burrowing animals, troops dig in and wait for a counter-attack, warily scanning the horizon for signs of the enemy. The earth protects them. They will sleep here, fitfully perhaps, in the mud and clay, snatching a hot meal when they can. Even in battle, soldiers must eat and sleep. They go to ground like the foxes and badgers and wait.

Soldiers are forever waiting. First the urgency, the haste, the flap; then the waiting. Waiting to be fed. Waiting to attack. Waiting to retreat. Waiting to be locked up. Waiting for release. War is full of excitement and danger. It is also full of tedium. Soldiers feel the pain of empty time. Marking time. Killing time. Yet there is never enough time for living, for freedom, for happiness. It is only in the waiting that time becomes bloated and heavy, weighing on the heart.

And the earth that protects receives them at last. The farmer and his women did not know the young man whose soul they pray for as they bury his body, tenderly, with flowers. They know only that he was a man who came with others to give them back their freedom. Moved by his sacrifice, they will not forget this day until they too are claimed by the earth.

'Common mother, thou,
Whose womb unmeasurable and infinite breast
Teems and feeds all . . .'

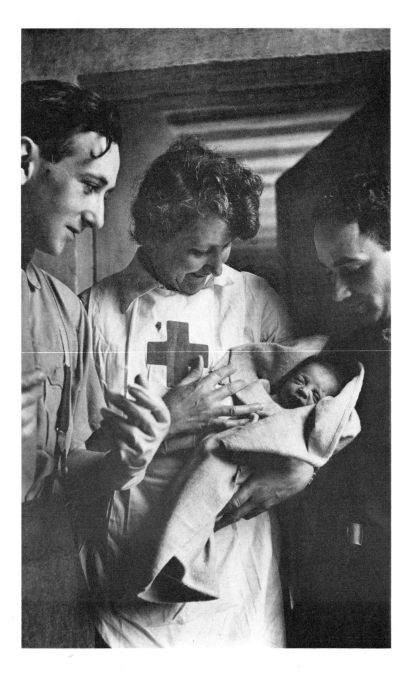

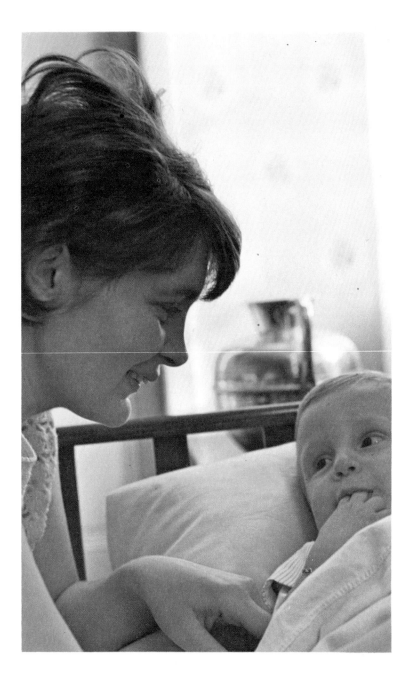

Life's rhythms persist while men fight. An American doctor and a Free French doctor and nurse assist at the birth of a French baby at Villons-les-Buissons. Twenty-five years later the baby, now a young woman, smiles at her own child.

Through a shattered village, the 17-pounder anti-tank gun is towed towards Caen. When the soldiers have gone, the people will come back and take up their lives again, patiently mending and restoring. The same street-scene frames the ancient riddle: Why did the chicken cross the road?

For, if thou sleep not, busy maggots eat
Thy brain, and all is dedicate to chaos.

Man confronts monster. This German Panther tank will
never fight again. But thrifty Normans can find other
uses for it. The same converted Panther is still at work.

Through orchards and back-roads, over a planned route,
invaders advance with their carriers and armour. Infantrymen
footslog it forward: there is no rest ahead.

A wounded prisoner glares defiance. A Hitler Youth member,
he is one of the lucky ones: few surrender.

It is human to take care of others. A nun strides, frowning, on her errand of mercy. Children take the baby for a ride . . .

. . . in streets where men carried their wounded. In motion, the jeep flies a conspicuous red cross. But note the rolled-up camouflage net in front. Parked, the jeep will be a sitting target; it is safer hidden.

With relentless persistence, British heavy artillery fires all night, hurling missiles of death into the distance.

There is stubborn fighting on the road to Caen. A Sherman tank churns past the tortured wreckage of another vehicle while, over the hill through the smoke, the infantry keeps moving on.

A soldier pauses before the Virgin and Holy Child in the rubble of the ancient church of Carpiquet on the fringes of Caen.

Here, on a Caen street, only a few hours ago, Bombardier E I Hill was buried where he fell. He came bringing destruction as the price of liberty, but a woman of the city brings flowers to his grave.

This is what it is to capture a
city. This is liberation.
Mop-up troops pick their
way through the ruins of
Caen, alert for snipers, mines,
boobytraps, tripwires,
falling masonry. Not much
hope of a night on the town
here.

The women work to keep life
going. Something can be
salvaged, if only to feed the
stove. Later, there will be
time for tears.

The church has been rebuilt, stone on stone;
the Virgin is invoked as in ancient times.

And the people of Caen, as they promised,
remember the liberators, honouring them every
48   year with a ceremony where Bombardier Hill fell.

A renewed city has flowed from the ruins,
thriving with the wealth of the European
community of former allies and enemies. The
sun shines, war and destruction have receded in
memory. Have the dark places of the heart
been conquered?

49

Free to go and come as they wish, people take
trains that run to predictable timetables, the
prosaic rhythms of peace. Partings and reunions
are commonplace, all in the day's living.

It was different then, in the wreckage after battle. A
moment of stillness as dazed prisoners and guard take the
weight off their feet.

With Caen—what's left of it—secure, the Allies are poised for a new thrust. Hitler has ordered his toughest Panzer formations forward in a massive counterattack. Allied air forces batter them to a standstill. Patton's Americans, already far inland at Le Mans, swing north in a lunge at Argentan. Canadian armour readies for a drive at the enemy flank in Falaise.

The earth returns. In the stillness, the rumble of a tractor is a distant echo of the faraway tumult of armour and battle-planes. Summer lengthens toward autumn and winter will come, but the seed will quicken in the earth and there will be other summers.

Quiet hours at Potigny, on the threshold of Falaise. Red, orange, yellow, green, blue, indigo, violet are the colours of the visible spectrum; to the eye of faith, a token of God's promise not to destroy man. But it is man who destroys man. Many soldiers died here when they were bombed accidentally by their own allies.

The gentle earth beckons with its blue distances, country of generous produce, mellow with bread and apples, butter and fragrant cheeses. Here soldiers came to harvest blood and steel and reap the holocaust.

In the grip of a passion stronger than the fear of death, hunter
and quarry play out their immemorial drama. A soldier lurks
in the hay. A victim lies dead beside the cigarette he never got to
smoke, his weapon and boots already carried off by the living.
Men have always hunted in the fields around Potigny and
Falaise. They still do, but no longer their own species.

The gallant equestrian in front of this church in Falaise represents William the Conqueror, a native of the town who once led a successful invasion in the other direction. Canadians finally captured Falaise on August 16 after some of the costliest fighting of the war.

The church at Rocquancourt, on the road to Falaise, that got in the way. Monsieur le curé, wearing a steel helmet, surveys the damage.

Part II

From Normandy to the Rhine

After discussions between Eisenhower, Montgomery, and Bradley, the Allied plan was now modified. Instead of driving on to the Seine, Patton was to turn north towards Argentan in a 'short hook' designed to make contact with the Canadians fighting south from Falaise and thus cut off the German force collected east of Avranches. On the night of 7–8 August the 2nd Canadian Corps, commanded by Lieut-General G G Simonds, attacked through the darkness towards Falaise, supported by a great blow from the RAF Bomber Command. The Germans here were in prepared positions, and though most of their armour had now moved west they fought grimly and skilfully. By the evening of 10 August the Canadian offensive had bogged down short of Falaise, after an advance of some nine miles. Another 'set-piece' attack had to be organized, but this could not go in for four days.

On the Canadians' right, the Second British Army was steadily pressing the Germans back west of Falaise; and by 12 August Patton's northward thrust had reached the vicinity of Argentan, only fifteen miles or so south of Falaise. The Germans were now caught in a pocket and were threatened with ruin if they could not escape through the narrowing gap that separated the Canadian and American armies. At this critical moment, however, Patton was stopped by orders from General Bradley, who, fighting by the book, feared disastrous confusion—Eisenhower, who agreed with him, used the phrase 'a calamitous battle between friends'—if the established boundary between the British and American army groups, which ran near Argentan, was not respected. The Germans in front of Patton, unlike those facing Crerar, were disorganized, and these orders probably had the result of considerably delaying the closing of the gap.

The second Canadian offensive against Falaise was launched in daylight on 14 August 'through fields of waving golden grain'. The ruined town fell to Crerar's men on the 16th. During the next three days the Allied air forces mercilessly hammered the hapless Germans struggling to get away to the eastward through the gap, and the roads were jammed with smashed and burning vehicles and dead men and horses. On the evening of the 19th the 1st Polish Armoured Division, fighting under the 2nd Canadian Corps, entered Chambois, south-east of Falaise. Simultaneously troops of the First US Army (commanded by General Courtney H Hodges since Bradley had taken command of an army group) came into the town from the other side. Thus the Falaise Gap was closed, but the next day witnessed desperate fighting as the Germans strove to break out of the encirclement. Only on 21 August did silence fall on the gap battle-field. The Battle of Normandy was over. Hitler's forces had suffered a shattering defeat. The Seventh German Army had been virtually destroyed; the Fifth Panzer Army had had tremendous losses. German casualties in Normandy numbered roughly 400,000 killed, wounded, and captured; the Allies' losses were only about half as many. The great Allied victory can be considered primarily Montgomery's. It was crowned on 25 August by the liberation of Paris, when General Jacques Leclerc's 2nd French Armoured Division drove into the capital.

The next phase was pursuit. Once their stubborn defence in Normandy was broken, the Germans fell back rapidly towards their own frontier, the remnants of their armies nevertheless still fighting fierce rearguard actions. Patton, balked at Argentan, had rushed on to the Seine, which he reached as early as 18–19 August. There was a possibility of another encirclement here, with the Americans sweeping down the river and cutting off the enemy retreating before the British and Canadians. The two Allied army groups made contact around Elbeuf on 25 August, but the Germans offered such determined resistance on the approaches to the lower Seine that Rouen fell to the Canadians only on the 30th. Once the Seine had been crossed this sort of opposition was no longer met, and the Second British Army, tearing north-eastward into Belgium, liberated Brussels on 3 September and Antwerp the following day. Eisenhower wrote on 2 September, 'All reports show that the enemy is routed and running on our entire front.' But the supply problem was suddenly serious. That day Patton's army reached the River Meuse, and was stopped there for want of gasoline.

While the battle of the Falaise Gap raged there had been developments far to the south. On 15 August General A M Patch's Seventh US Army landed on the Mediterranean coast of France. It included many French troops and the Canadian-American First Special Service Force. The British and American strategists had had a very long wrangle over the operation ('Anvil', later re-christened 'Dragoon'), which the British did not like. Whatever its strategic value, it at least met little opposition from the Germans. Patch's men advanced rapidly up the Rhone valley and joined hands with Patton's on 11 September. From 25 September the French force in this Allied right sector operated as the First French Army, commanded by General de Lattre de Tassigny.

With the Germans in full retreat after Normandy, the Allied commanders in the European theatre fell into a famous disagreement over the strategy for finishing off the war. Eisenhower, apparently following a plan drawn up before D-Day by three British members of his staff, proposed to advance against Germany on two lines, north and south of the Ardennes forest. Montgomery was, perhaps, anxious to hold the limelight in spite of the fact that he was now merely a commander of one of three army groups (Eisenhower had taken direct control of all ground forces on 1 September). At any rate, the British leader argued for 'one really powerful and full-blooded thrust towards Berlin'—in the north, and under his own command. All the limited battle supplies available in the theatre were to be placed at the disposal of Montgomery's army group; the rest of the Allied force would be able to do nothing but watch helplessly while the left wing slugged it out with the enemy on the North German plain. Eisenhower, with his position as Supreme Commander and the big American battalions to back him, won the argument; but not before he had compromised to the extent of allowing Montgomery to attempt a major airborne operation designed to put the Allies across the Lower Rhine at Arnhem. This was a narrow but tragic failure (17–26 September). The great bridge across the Waal at Nijmegen, and the crossing of the Maas at Grave, were successfully seized and held; but the Second Army failed to make effective contact with the 1st British Airborne Division, clinging gallantly to the bridge at Arnhem. During the same period Hodges' army was fighting its way through the German frontier defences towards Aachen, and the First Canadian Army, with the 1st British Corps under its command, was besieging and taking the formidably fortified Channel Ports—Le Havre, Boulogne, and Calais. The Cap Gris Nez batteries, which had long harassed the citizens of Dover, also fell to Canadian attack. The British 51st (Highland) Division had had the satisfaction of taking St. Valéry, where the bulk of the division had been forced to surrender in the Dunkirk campaign of 1940; and the 2nd Canadian Division had occupied Dieppe, where it had been decimated in the famous and bloody raid of August 1942. Many old bills were coming due.

There were powerful arguments for Montgomery's plan for the offensive against Germany, even though it involved attacking with only a portion of the Allied forces; the importance of keeping the enemy on the run, the possibility of exploiting the victory that had been won to finish the war in 1944, the propriety of taking great risks for so great a result. Field-Marshal Montgomery has argued ever since that he was right, and military students will discuss the controversy till the end of time. But it is questionable whether, with the Allied armies still being maintained over the long haul from the Normandy beaches, and the Channel ports not yet available, the logistical basis existed for a successful thrust into Germany in September 1944. Arnhem demonstrated that the Germans were still extremely dangerous. Good judges have felt that Montgomery would have been wiser to devote all available resources to opening the great inland port of Antwerp, an object to which he gave comparatively low priority until Eisenhower gave him a very direct order on 13 October.

There is bitter house-to-house fighting in Falaise. Infantry
follow a Sherman tank through the debris; death lurks at every
corner and every window.

Some paid a ghastly price for inexperience. But a man can age
years in a single day of battle, once all his nerves have learned the
simple rule; kill, or be killed.

Houses are no longer houses in the town, abandoned to the soldiers. They are strongpoints, nests of resistance. No one knocks at doors here; they are kicked open to receive a grenade or a burst of fire.

'Bang! you're dead!' But no one lies twisted on this street in
Falaise when this game is over.

Agony of a city. Soldiers inch forward relentlessly through the streets of Falaise. The town square is in ruins.

Battle has raged through the town, rolling on to consume the trapped enemy. Miraculously, the faces of children appear, like flowers, in windows and doorways. Homesick troops make much of them.

Five years later stonemasons are still rebuilding the shattered town square.

69

The smoke has hardly cleared when the good sisters return
to tidy up. There's much to be done, one cannot begin
too soon.

Its town square restored, Falaise has long since returned to its quiet ways, minding its own business. And other people's.

71

After the killing there is untidiness outside this restaurant.
The retreating Germans and Allies came by on their way to the
Seine. Five years afterwards the chef reminisces with a
gendarme; German divisional signs remain.

Prosperity puts a new face on the building. And the young—do
they know what happened here? It was all so long ago.

Allies get together at Elbeuf on the Seine, exchanging jokes and cigarettes. Good-natured and humorous, the soldiers are ready for any sort of violence at a moment's notice—witness the field-dressings stashed in helmet-nets.

No longer an obstacle but a life-giving artery, the river flows tranquil under many bridges.

Today the big risk is that the light may change too quickly.

Engineers labour to get the army across the Seine in pursuit of the enemy. A half-track vehicle crosses on a ferry.

Within hours the sappers have a pontoon bridge ready,
and an audience arrives to watch the traffic pass, the symbol
of their liberation. Armour and transport can roll forward
once more, striking for Rouen and northward to Dieppe.

Prospect of Rouen, with its ancient cathedral and its young women moving in the sunlight.

Maquis partisans, after their long resistance, come into the open to lead in the liberation of Rouen.

Allied engineers construct a mighty bridge in front of the cathedral. A dreaded German 88 mm gun stands in the foreground.

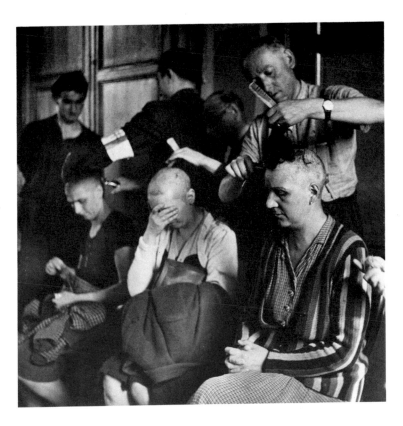

Freed from Nazi oppression, Rouen gives way to revenge. Women who collaborated with the enemy have their heads shaved. It is not only defeat that twists men's hearts: victory can be ugly too, for hatred dies hard.

For some women in Rouen today, too much hair is not enough.

A trim seaside place, Dieppe. The grass seems to grow to municipal specifications here in Canada Park. Hardy swimmers dip in the chill waters of the Channel where the English ferries come and go.

Canadians re-entered Dieppe without fighting, in sharp
contrast to the agony of the sea-borne raid of August, 1942,
whose dearly bought lessons were to prove so valuable to the
Allies two years later.

Victorious Germans took this picture of carnage on the assault
beach at Dieppe in 1942. A tank-landing craft burns, two tanks
that untracked themselves by making sharp turns on the stony
beach are disabled, the dead lie face upward.

The same beach warmed by the same sun.

Sergeant G R MacDonald was among the liberators. He breeds samoyeds now.

Sergeant MacDonald in action, giving first aid—
to the dismay of one squeamish onlooker.

The offensive has moved on to free the Channel ports, leaving
prisoners and dead in rear. Prisoners are put to work burying
the dead, heavily guarded by maquis partisans. It pleases them
to see their former oppressors at this work.

A strongpoint falls at Cap Gris Nez. Soldiers trudge
through a desert of chalk and lunar desolation.

Telegraph-wires hum in the sea breeze, a farmer spreads manure, the crops grow, and the same strongpoints have become a bijou residence—with 14 foot walls!

They have always entertained the troops.

And who are these men? How did they get in here?
Their names are Wayne and Shuster and they
entertain the troops.

Even the artillery have learned to cope with the mud.
These men are winching out a 3·7 inch anti–aircraft gun.

Sea-birds follow the farmer's tractor over the same earth, now tended lovingly. The powers of sky and soil join in fertility.

What could be more satisfying than a walking race in the cobbled streets of Arras? These citizens can show the young fellows a thing or two.

The liberators roll into Arras in their Shermans. Have they
come to stay? Will the town be smashed in a counter-
attack? The people are not sure, yet, what to feel, fearing
disappointment, remembering 1914–18.

Sergeant H A Marshall was a sniper in those days, handsome and deadly. Today, wielding a broom, he's the terror of a Calgary curling rink.

The retreating enemy sowed mines behind him. Advancing soldiers with mine-detecting gear move warily forward to clear a road.

Marking a road is less dangerous now. But French roads are safe only during the lunch hour when everyone is eating.

Part III
Through Holland and Germany

General Dempsey's Second British Army, as already noted, had taken Antwerp on 4 September. But both banks of the River Scheldt below it remained in enemy hands, and until they were cleared the port—the one gateway through which the supplies needed for the conquest of Germany could certainly reach the Allied armies in adequate quantities—could not be used. The task of clearance fell to the Canadians. It was thoroughly nasty. The lands along the Scheldt, in great part reclaimed from the sea, flat, muddy, and in many places flooded, were the worst battlefield imaginable; and the Germans, knowing the importance of the ground they held, fought with even more than their usual resolution. The operation's priority, we have seen, was low; air support in particular was inadequate. The divisions of the 2nd Canadian Corps had heavy losses in the painful struggle on both sides of the West Scheldt. The culminating episode was the seaborne assault on the very strong island of Walcheren by British Royal Marine Commandos, an affair marked by the gallantry of the light craft of the Royal Navy's support squadron. The Battle of the Scheldt may be said to have begun on 2 October; it ended only on 8 November, by which time the minesweepers were already clearing the river. The first convoy reached Antwerp on the 28th.

While the Allies were preparing an offensive to evict the Germans from the country between the Maas and the Rhine, preparatory to striking across the Rhine into the heart of Germany, Hitler—again it was his own strategic conception—played his last card. On 16 December 1944 his armies, aided and covered by dirty winter weather, lunged forward through the snowy Ardennes at the thinnest portion of the American line, taking the First US Army wholly by surprise. A deep penetration was made before hard fighting by the Americans held the attack. In retrospect it seems evident that the dictator would have been wiser to hold back his forces to resist our coming thrust across the Rhine, for the thousands of soldiers he lost in the bitter Ardennes battle—the 'Battle of the Bulge'—could not be replaced.

There was still to be fierce fighting west of the Rhine. Delayed by the Germans' Ardennes attack, the offensive between the Maas and the Rhine, remembered as the Battle of the Rhineland, was launched by the First Canadian Army (reinforced by most of the divisions that normally fought under the Second British Army) on 8 February. The ground troops were supported by a great concentration of British and US air power. The Germans, on their own soil now, continued to resist fiercely, feeding into the grinder formations they had no hope of ever replacing. Again ground conditions were terrible. Eisenhower wrote to Crerar afterwards, 'Probably no assault in this war has been conducted under more appalling conditions of terrain.' The plan called for a converging attack by General W H Simpson's Ninth US Army which would draw off some of the enemy divisions that would otherwise be used against General Crerar; but the Germans scotched that for the moment by opening the dams on the Roer River and producing flooding which delayed the American attack until 23 February. In the meantime the enemy facing the Canadians was reinforced from the US front. The British and Canadian divisions fought grimly forward through the Reichswald and Hochwald forests and across the flooded areas along the Rhine. Once the Ninth Army got going things went faster. By 10 March the surviving Germans had been driven back across the great river and one more bloody battle was at an end.

After the Battle of the Rhineland the worst was over; for the German Wehrmacht had not the means of making a second recovery similar to the one it had contrived after Normandy. The German forces in the west could no longer offer the sort of resistance the Allies had met in the early months. Of the men who had fought so staunchly then, many hundreds of thousands were dead, prisoners, or disabled. And in the east the Russians, who, be it remembered, had always pinned down not less than two-thirds of the German Army, were rolling inexorably forward towards Vienna, Prague, and Berlin.

There was, however, some further disagreement between the Western Allies themselves. At the end of January 1945 General Eisenhower assured the Combined Chiefs of Staff that he intended to 'advance across the Rhine in the north with maximum strength', thus indicating, to the satisfaction of the British, that the main effort would be made in Montgomery's area. The Second British Army, with some Canadians under command, assaulted across the Rhine on 23 March, meeting only moderate resistance. By this time both the First and Third US Armies had already made lodgements beyond the river, the former with the aid of the famous Remagen bridge. A few days later Eisenhower apparently changed his mind and informed Montgomery that the Ninth US Army which had been operating under him would be withdrawn; the main effort would now be made by General Bradley's army group in the centre, and Montgomery's task would be to protect Bradley's left flank. Moreover, whereas earlier the Supreme Commander had seen Berlin as the great Allied objective, he now took the view that it was no longer particularly important. Mr. Churchill argued that 'from a political standpoint' it was desirable for the Western Allies to beat the Soviet troops to Berlin and Prague; but the American political and military authorities could not be moved. The Russians were allowed to capture the German capital and to liberate Czechoslovakia's. Americans have been regretting this ever since.

In the final phase the First and Ninth US Armies encircled the great industrial area of the Ruhr (meeting beyond it on 1 April); over 300,000 prisoners were taken in the Ruhr pocket. The Third and Seventh US Armies and the First French Army cleared Southern Germany. Nuremberg fell on 20 April, Munich on the 30th. On 25 April advanced troops of the First US Army met the Russians at Torgau on the Elbe and Germany was cut in two. In the north the Second British Army drove on to Bremen and Hamburg; on 2 May its spearhead—the Canadian Parachute Battalion riding on the tanks of the Scots Greys—reached the waters of the Baltic at Wismar.

Hereabouts all opposition had ceased; what the Germans most wanted now was for the British and Americans to advance as far east as possible, occupying territory that otherwise would fall to the dreaded Russians.

The First Canadian Army was still operating on the extreme left of the Allied line as it had been from the beginning. The 1st Canadian Corps, which arrived from Italy only a few weeks before the end, was advancing on Utrecht and Amsterdam, but the advance was stayed in mid-April. What amounted to a truce was reached with the German administration in this area and our troops stood fast while arrangements were made to send in food to the starving Dutch population. Meanwhile the 2nd Canadian Corps cleared the enemy from the northern Netherlands and fought forward across the soggy German plain to Oldenburg. Here the Germans had no Russians coming up behind them; and the Canadians were still meeting fierce if disorganized opposition when the German command surrendered its forces in Holland, north-west Germany, and Denmark to Field-Marshal Montgomery on 4 May.

On 30 April Adolf Hitler had killed himself in his beleaguered bunker in Berlin. On 7 May General Jodl surrendered all German forces at Eisenhower's headquarters at Rheims. The Supreme Allied Commander reported the event to the Combined Chiefs of Staff with soldierly brevity and justifiable pride: 'The mission of this Allied force was fulfilled at 0241, local time, May 7th 1945.' As for the fighting soldiers, the diarist of the Queen's Own Rifles of Canada spoke for all of them: 'There is no celebration but everybody is happy.'

As the offensive thrusts through Belgium into Holland, water once more becomes the soldier's element. A vehicle and trailer come to grief by the flooded Scheldt estuary near Antwerp.

Amphibious vehicles swim troops and supplies over the estuary.

A 'DUKW' vehicle is still in use—for pleasure.

The soldiers are forever soaked as they advance in the damp
autumn air of Holland. The Dutch have won this country from
the sea and now the Canadians are winning it back from the Germans.

Between mud and water (staked to prevent glider-landings)
a column of Shermans slowly advances through North
Beveland. Allied air forces have cleared the skies of enemy
planes, and there is no fear of bombing or strafing.

Bridge, canal, windmill, ducks. Holland has been like this
for centuries.

In this watery maze—staked, now, for fish-nets—the
soldiers found and defeated the enemy.

Sky and water; trees and water; mist and water.
And water.

Say wisdom is a silver fish,
And love a golden hook.
JAY MACPHERSON

The enemy drew back among the canals, leaving roads and fields lethal with mines and booby-traps. Soldiers hit the ground as a mine explodes. Another soldier delicately disarms a mine he has unearthed.

Artillery batters away at the enemy positions.

Floods have been drained, the roads are wide open, all is bright and clean in picture-book Holland.

Signposts were still in place as the Shermans rumbled forward, across the flatlands of Zeeland and the channelled mouths of the Rhine.

Engineers have thrown a pontoon bridge across the Beveland
Canal beside the one the Germans destroyed in their retreat.
A 25-pounder crosses safely.

The same bridge today.

Looming soft in the mist is the bridge at Nijmegen. A squad of Dutch soldiers amble in the foreground. No danger threatens from the sky.

Captured before the enemy could blow it up, the Nijmegen bridge over the Rhine is a valuable prize. The Allies cross at once to press toward Arnhem, where Montgomery has landed airborne forces in an attempt to seize a Rhine crossing and bring victory in 1944.

The Germans boobytrap even their dead. In the Hochwald Forest, south of the Rhine, a soldier approaches a corpse with a mine-detector.

A path through the Hochwald Forest. Under brush has grown over the places where men bled and died.

The Allies have driven the Germans back into their own country, and once again it is a time of bitter house-to-house fighting. This is what is left of a German town after the battle.

122

An armoured car at the medieval gates of Xanten
is metamorphosed over twenty-five years into a
sleek Mercedes-Benz.

Now it is the Germans' turn to become refugees. But is that strapping young man really a civilian in flight? Or a soldier who has thrown away his uniform?

The wheel of fortune turns and Hitler feels that Germany should perish with him. This German woman is homeless now, but she is still more fortunate than some of Hitler's earlier victims.

These children do not remember the days of bitterness.
But as they grow older and read their history books, they
will ask their elders : why ?

Why ? Why did a generation go mad and set Europe in
flames ? The baby does not know, her young mother does
not know. The grandparents who lived through it—
there are times when they cannot believe it happened.

Refugees, refugees. It is the age of the DP, the displaced
person, the deported, the homeless, the stateless. Some will
find new homes across the Atlantic; but there are others
who will be turned away from frontier after frontier.

The soldiers hardly glance at these refugees. When the
tables are turned on the aggressors, there is little sympathy
for them. But they are all victims, the refugees *and* the soldiers.

There is a world of affluence and open frontiers for these young
Germans.
For the Hitler Youth, there had been a diet of elderly rubbish,
racism, regimentation, and brass bands. It brought them death,
glory, captivity. And a long aftermath of shame.

The end may be in sight, the result known; but the fighting is
not over. Once more the soldiers advance through floods.
It is as if the world is drowning.

Infantrymen are used to water, and this beats foot slogging any day. 'You'd pay thousands for this in civvy street' they tell each other as they take to the water again.

One more river . . . there is always another river to cross, a hard march on foot, another battle, another river. The soldiers can sense victory now. They fight harder than ever. And some pass over the river in Zutphen, where in 1586 Sir Philip Sidney was also mortally wounded.

And here, with almost reckless exuberance, they cross the Ijssel, northernmost channel of the Rhine. Today the river is a busy thoroughfare of European commerce—peaceful but polluted.

136

137

Dutiful but without hope, the enemy defends a line.
Soldiers move to a position behind a hedge, poised to fight,
bellies to the ground.

Others take cover along a wall, ready to move forward.
Some may have to die when victory is already won.

It is all over now. The generals confront one another in a
ceremony of formal surrender. General Foulkes receives
the submission of his adversaries from General Blaskowitz
in a room in the town hall at Wageningen. The Third
Reich has collapsed. The Russians storm into Berlin.

As the vanquished stream
home over the dyke across
the Zuider Zee, victors and
victims are already facing
the massive work of
reconstruction. One more
world war has been fought;
but Japan fights on, soon to
be blasted by weapons that
make this European conflict
seem like the last convulsion
of a chivalrous past.

In peace there's nothing so becomes a man
As modest stillness and humility . . .